EVEN THE SEA

Even the Sea

Poems

Eleanor Livingstone

RED SQUIRREL PRESS

First published by Red Squirrel Press in 2010,
this new and revised edition published in 2023
36 Elphinstone Crescent
Biggar
South Lanarkshire
ML12 6GU
www.redsquirrelpress.com

Layout, design and typesetting by Gerry Cambridge
e: gerry.cambridge@btinternet.com

A CIP catalogue record for this book is available
from the British Library.

ISBN: 978 1 913632 48 9

Red Squirrel Press is committed to a sustainable future.
This publication is printed in the UK by Imprint Digital
using Forest Stewardship Council certified paper.
https://digital.imprint.co.uk

Contents

v. *now it starts*

even metaphor

i.

nothing soft lasts here
the sea cuts clean to the bone
a knife in each hand

Shorehead

Past a row of taxis
behind the bus terminus
where seagulls eye up
takeaway wrappers

signs declare—*Leven Bay
Fish Bar and Restaurant,
Real Spice, Currys, Pizzas,
Kebabs, Home* ....*very*

in occasional neon,
while on the back
of a mini-bus parked
in the (deli)very heart of it

*Mac Tours—real Scots
showing you the real Scotland.*

Silly Bitch

Like the dog on the beach
whose owner keeps shouting
stay down

something in her
leaps when she sees him
and bounds off into the surf

while he still holds
that promise of pebble
gleaming with salt water

clenched in his fist.

How to Watch a Seagull Die

The parent birds must build a nest
on the brick cliffs of our chimney stack
three hundred yards from the promenade,
and the first we'll know of it will be
when two pompoms of grey fluff
land on the half roof overlooked
by the photocopier and the fax machine.

And though the mother gull
dives at us, squawking every time
she sees us dart from car to office door,
we watch as spring warms into summer
and the fledglings sleep and peck and flap their way
into adulthood, growing sleek grey feathers,
discarding the fluff of their infant lives.

Eyeing us through the glass, impatiently they pace
the five square yards of roof, measuring by hops
and runs and wingspans, readying for take-off.
Then this fine morning we arrive to find one
not asleep but huddled, less, trying again
and again to shake his fractious feathers
into place; and again. All day

while the fax machine bleeps
and the photocopier hums away
we watch from our side of the window,
one eye on the clock, knowing that at five
we'll pull down the blinds, switch off
the photocopier and leave the office,
avoiding the eye of the waiting mother bird.

On Hearing Poems Read
in English and Gaelic

In the trees gathered
beyond the window, birds
who also sing in different voices
listen as the lines and verses
rush in over rocks and pebbles;
listen to the susurration: words
wash over sand and shingle
as the tide slips out.

Good Friday, 5 pm

Gulls at the water's edge cease their squabbling
and fly away. Empty crisp bags bustle out of sight.
An aeroplane's thin white drone is swallowed

by cloud and the catch in each dog's breath
passes beyond reach. Children's voices
fade into tomorrow while the sun retreats

behind the old beach pavilion, leaving a chill
in the stones of the sea wall, in bones
half buried at the high water mark.

Storm

Half a mile beyond the village
summer rain leaps out.

It hurls down buckets full
of noise; and breathless

laughter chases them
along the disused railway track

the only movement
in the landscape

other than the teeming rain.
Even the sea holds still

while they beat on.
Wet sandals on the sleepers

find a rhythm;
licks of hair drip down.

The taste of rain
is everything to come.

Rain

For He [...] sendeth rain on the just and on the unjust.
—Matthew 5 : 45

All summer it surprised
every forecast and event,
chenille blankets on the line

as drookit as spaniels' lugs
when thunder cracked open
the odd hopeful afternoon.

On warm nights, single spies:
one. Ten-second pause. Another
sweating in the streetlamps' glare.

And now as wasps die off
it falls even from clear skies,
a wedding shower of sixpences.

Bare-headed, we stare upwards
searching for a hint of cloud.

Dysart at Dusk

The percussion
of boats on water

metal gang-planks
feeling the wind's chill

wave after wave
coming home to roost

cooing from holes
in the harbour wall

nets gathering in
the echoes of the day.

One More River

when the low sun
walks on water

boats with sails
turn into kites

Harbour

And if you should go back
to stand out there alone
salt soaked to the bone

call me then: don't speak,
just let my tongue taste salt
when I lick the phone.

It's Not

as cold as it sounds
as deep as it lies
as sweet as it reaches up
as sour as it falls
as sharp as it measures
as square as it breaks
across the ears
as out of sympathy
as it stains the creases
of your palms
as careful as a flood
as far sighted as salt
on an autumn day
as close as this

News

Reliant first on word of mouth
and then the penny post, later
the death-watch tick of the telegraph,
it had its work cut out to reach us.

In the days of Barnum
it learned to be a trapeze artist
balanced on the high wire
announced by a fanfare.

Still, there was a whole world
where we could be safe: on trains,
in shops, lost in a forest of city blocks,
on the wide sweep of empty beaches

where sand dunes and concrete
fortifications held it at bay. Now
the only refuge from bad news
is in art, in libraries or galleries

patrolled by shushing librarians
and silent notices; and sometimes
in the windy lee of tall buildings
before they fall.

The Witchfinder's Daughter

So when you reach for me in bed each night,
your hand on my bare thigh, I make myself
go tense, and listen as you sigh, a sound
as soft as a kiss let loose in the air.

You turn your back and I can only see
white skin, a scattering of fine dark hair,
a stillness in the hollow round the root
of your spine.
                     It will be in a hidden

or tender spot; and so night after night
I keep on testing, making you expose
your secret places. Making you cry proves

nothing; but when I stick my needle in
and you turn round at last to look at me
without a sound, then I know I've struck home.

ii.

a Sunday in June
no bees in sight but listen
to the tree humming

Increasing the Volume

Too hot to sleep, I open
the bathroom window
and lean against a white
coolness of sink.

My wrists and arms
reddened by days of sun
throb from the rush
of cold tap water.

It's 3.15 am, early June.
Outside one bird
alone in the almost dark
sings vibrato.

Foghorn

the reality is a low
mournful sound

keening over the water
finding us in bright, still
sunlight

here and there, in ones
and twos, in small groups,
we pause, turn as if pulled
by compass force

we peer through gaps
between white washed walls
and pantiled roofs

through the glare
which shears off knife-edged
waves and rocks
into blankness

                            we hear you
we hear you

                       hands cupped
against foreheads, eyes shaded,
scanning a sudden silence

Undertow

sea light dawns in the room
waking me early   to drift
with pages   open

bare thighs seek out shallows
of cool sheet   feet lift as the tide
comes in again   the languor of July

an undertow pulling me down
through folds of quilt   words
slip from fingers   images

cut loose   float away

Dandelion Clock

August again.
That slant of light
angles to catch
an hour which lies
still round and perfect
in my hand. Hush—
not a breath.
The faintest sigh
and minutes fly off
dazzling the sun.
Hush. Close your eyes.

Drouth

nails rough edged
from scrabbling at rock
with seeds so small

I'm trusting they exist
spitting
               on the thought of them

coaxing life
into hairline cracks
blood from raw fingers

the only watering in

Ground Bass

While bars of sun and shadow
blow across the graveyard

sheltered by a small headstone
a pair of black gloves shiver
on the grass, piano fingers

poised between the chorus
which could sweep them up
into the wild blue skies of autumn

and the suck and drone
of the heavy loam below.

Old Dogs

are kinder
than old men,
their ears
still velvet soft
and kissable.

The Travellers' Dog

My mother refused to give them money
for drink but buttered half a loaf of bread
instead, while their dog licked at my bare toes.
One wild night years later they set up camp
in the sorry huddle of grass and trees
across the road, their voices reaching me
despite the racket of the night, talking
arguing—even singing, off and on.

I lay in bed, only a few thin yards of wind
and rain between me and them, and pulled
the quilt over my head against the thought
of the old dog lying on the grass, cold earth
beneath him, rain on his back, worn collar
wet round his neck: our door, locked and bolted.

The Soul

His ears lift up
tugged by wires from above.
He waits, nose wet and shining,
sinews in his legs and back
straining towards the darkness
beyond the station lights.

Each hair of his coat is ready,
in full course, *courant*, tail stiff,
eyes—oh, his eyes—
ears tugged,
                    tugged
by those wires, four paws
holding the platform down

until at last the train arrives
and hope flickers this way and that.
His eyes, with tiny nervous pulses,
scan each face. Each face passes.
Pass friend. He waits. He waits
on guard, a soul unguarded.

At this cold juncture,
late at night,
beyond all rational hope

he waits.

Night Watch

They placed him on his side
a silhouette against the pillow, skin
stretched over long thin bones,

his limbs in constant spasm, as if
he might still jerk himself awake
like a dog chasing dream hares

leaping fences; and I followed
through that cold February night,
covering wordless mile after mile,

a whole country mapped
between us, fields and mountains,
lochs and burns, half frozen rivers

and an outline up ahead, white
on white, passing out of sight.

iii.

moments framed
by empty flashes

older heads
thrown into silhouette

Once Upon a Time

propped up by pillows
in my parents' bed
cheeks flushed

while my brother
played with toy cars
on the linoleum borders

of our small world,
I was so happy
I could hardly breathe.

Learning to Swim

lift up your feet!
   they all shout
      but sharp waves

      come at me
    from every angle
one and then another

fierce with light
    midday sun on water
       the width of the sky

      and salty spit
    filling my mouth
the horizon a thin rope

lift up your feet!
    they shout again
       in their element

      the only safety
    sand gripped
between cold toes

to hold the sea still
    lift up your feet!
      they shout

      when it's all I can do
    to keep them firmly
on the ground

The Deep End

The older boys are on it at once
finding their balance on the lower levels
then moving upwards; and one by one
the younger or more timid of us follow,

dropping off the springboard like stones,
pushing back up through wide echoing water;
then jumping, arms reaching out,
heels kicking.
                  As the hours go by

we venture up and further up, board
by board, foot by damp footprint, at last
daring the high dive, wet knees trembling
in the hill top air, panting from the climb,

stomachs hollow beneath nylon costumes,
little creatures closer to God, our arms
which next day will boast constellations
of tiny purple stars, waving, waving,

the pool chlorine blue and welcoming below
while we're up here almost touching heaven,
on top of everything, the world at our feet
just waiting for us to jump.

The Bridge

Remember the tree over the ravine
in the Serpie Woods where we used to play
on rope swings, to leap from sloping shelves of rock;
where we dared each other to walk across
the mossy green length of that awkward bridge
from childhood to our anxious older selves—

how some of us got scared about half-way
from there to here and swayed above the drop;
and one girl slithered to a stop, astride
the trunk, with boulders and the burn ten feet
below, thighs gripping tight, arms wrapped around;
and while the rest of us looked on with scorn,

she clung on there forever, unable
to go back, and unable to go on.

A Half-Taken Breath

Beyond ruined houses and a past
eroded by salt and marram grass
stretch miles of sand dunes
where as kids we hurled ourselves
into space, legs and rebel cries
suspended in the air, landing

spread-eagled in cotton shorts
and bare legs, winded but alive.

On August evenings years later
under cover of dark we returned
stumbling in and out of rabbit holes
to find the sand sun-warmed, soft
and far enough removed for us
to lie as still and silent as the sea

but for fingers finding buttons
and the racket of our hearts.

1973

Summer that year
when every night
was a party

blades of grass
shrugged off haircuts
and danced along

to the soft sounds
of cotton, cheesecloth
embroidered nightstock

windows open,
fence posts tie-dyed
by the evening sun

honeysuckled air
warm with riffs
of jasmine and rose

a field of barley
swaying to the music
as 'Sylvia' played on.

What We Called 'Barbecue'

Marram grass and the odd dead sheep.
A sweet smell, smoke in the air.

No food, no fire. Lager ring-pulls
flying off into the night to catch

a star or two, moonlight, perhaps,
and just enough luck to keep us upright

till we found our way home, this side or that
of midnight curfews, to face parents

with sand in our hair, mint on our breath,
clothes smelling of rabbit. *Barbecue,* we said.

Our Birthday

The joint celebration
was almost like Christmas,

opening cards and presents,
cutting just one cake,
the same old jokes, year

after year, carolling
'happy birthday to us!'
off-key at family gatherings

until Dad discovered
how to stop getting older,
left me to party on alone,

trying to blow out
with a single breath
those stupid everlasting candles,

the cake half naked
with only my name on it.

Bluebells

—for Jed

That evening we first met
my arms were full of them.
Embarrassed bunches
hung their heads quietly.
I clutched them to my chest
hands sticky with their milk
as I tried to hide my pink
in the coolness of their blue.

And now it's May again
though thirty years have passed.
These days I blush less easily—
but Letham Glen's aglow!
An avenue of flowering trees
holds parasols above our heads;
soft almond blossom showers
on us as sunlight filters through

and further up the path
the banks are steep with bluebells
row on row, a whole massed
choir of them, but now I know
not to pick wild flowers, so hand-
in-hand we stand beside them.
Nothing matters for the moment
but the bluebells, me and you.

July Evening

you're behind me in the room
busy with music
every window in the house

open
                  when a sudden gust
comes from nowhere

catches the trees
unaware, lifts branches
like a summer skirt

or an orchestra rising as one
for applause

while all my paperwork
stirs a breath's height off the desk,
the windows buck

and somewhere in the house
one slams shut
like a bolt

A Thousand Nights

Returning after midnight
to the warm glow
of one hall light left on

and a house barely awake,
the fridge humming
to itself

I pass through walls,
a ghost revisiting
my former life,

undress in the cool
darkness of the bedroom
and slip into bed

where your hand
reaches out and pulls me
back into the present.

Sic Transit

Beyond this upstairs room, those blinds,
a roof top with an aerial, the leafy
tree which neighbours it are silhouettes
against a backdrop of soon darker blue,
while—motionless, to all appearances—
we stand and watch the creamy harvest moon
back-lit sliding across the southern sky
where Artemis has autumn in her sights.

The moon is moving fast tonight, but not alone.
That roof top where she balances; the cloud
she hides behind a moment there; each leaf
about to fall from that birch tree; and you
and I, drawn to this window by the light
that shines on us—we're also passing by.

Tortoise

As you get older, he says
teeth grinning in the dark
before he rolls straight back
into oblivion, *you just
don't need as much.*

Exhausted after hours
trying to wrestle sleep
from tangled sheets, I'd like
to kick his sleeping butt
right out the bed.

But in the darkness
louder than the ticking clock
I hear old age, its shuffling feet
and laboured breath, slow but steady
catching up with both of us.

'50'

It hung around in corners
half deflated, long after the party
you didn't want was over.

Now it occupies
the middle ground between us
till we kick it out of sight.

Just watch. Some day the breeze
will waft it through an open door
and off that wrinkled bag of wind will go

careering over molehills
with little running jumps
growing smaller, smaller all the time

and we'll be chasing after it
as fast as creaking joints allow.

After the Fall

I lie awake.
You curl towards me
sound asleep, half
of two spoons. I move
a hand but can't reach you
find only sheet, the place
my hips should fill. I twist
and groan and grip the bed
until your sleeping knees
caress the back of mine
with knobbly tenderness.
The space between us
is still warm.

The Moment

In about half an hour we'll leave
this bookshop café

> *In a few years*
> *you'll be leaving home*

but meantime we joke
about this man's woolly hat
that woman's pile of books
tipping over

> *when we leave the bookshop*
> *it will still be raining*

as we laugh and hush
each other over plates
all crummy with pastry flakes

> *below the table there's only*
> *one small umbrella between us*

we sit back full of chocolate
twists, savouring the dregs
of latte and orange smoothie

> *and the rain will mess up*
> *your fringe and our day*

in the Ladies we check make-up
and hair; squeezed side by side

the puddles will soak up
and darken the legs of your jeans
like a litmus test for acid

we turn one last time, smile
at our reflections, lopsided
in the mirror; unaware

> *you will hate me long*
> *before we reach home*

we touch up lipstick
and gloss, turn again
smile.

Textual Analysis

Once upon a time
when you were three or four, for weeks
(perhaps because of the dog's face
on the cover) you insisted on falling asleep
with a library copy of *Woof!* in your arms.
You were too young to understand the text
or even have it read to you, but every morning
I'd find it snuggled warm under the covers.

Before *Woof!* and after, there had been
and would be, other books which—
if laid dog-eared end to end—
could have reached our local library
and back again: board books; all the bears
big and brown and Bramwell; bears
who couldn't sleep; bears in pyjamas
or Wellington boots; *Heidi;* the Topsy
who never grew up, and Tim. Even
the odd middle-aged Famous Five
or Castle of Adventure
fallen out of an earlier childhood.
We spelled out the words together.

You still fall asleep with a book
on your chest—but when I make your bed
these mornings, I find tangled in the covers
The Coming of the Third Reich
or *A Streetcar Named Desire*
and the words you don't understand
are 'autarchy' and 'monocausal',
beyond the scope of my dictionary—
they have to be looked up online.

The boy who turned into a dog
has run off into the night, and the girl
who hugged that book to sleep
is off on her own adventure.

The Snowman

A week later, we awoke to skies as blue
as Canada, a new whiteness everywhere;
and because life must go on, etc, and you
at not quite two and a half years old
were too young to understand anyway,
we went out to build your first snowman
helped by neighbours and their older kids
while our dog chased after snowballs.

In the photograph, you're all happed up—
an Inuit doll in navy hooded coat, boots,
mittens, scarf looped twice around below
those shining eyes, button nose *rosie bright*,
the dog's dark muzzle icicled with snow;
and my eyes still water at all that white.

iv.

you take the bend seamlessly
seamlessly the bend takes you

Cold Start

Dishes drip quietly in racks.
Morning spins in the machine
with one eye on the clock

as leashes are unclipped,
dogs shake their heads, ears
pistol-snap and the day takes off.

Beam or Mote?

Late February on the road
north out of Pittenweem

fields rise and dip,
stark brown and ready.

Trees point at colours
that bend the sky.

Don't look! you say—
Watch the road!

I drive on, a whole rainbow
in the corner of my eye.

Still

Not crow, eyes calculating
my speed, the distance, his time.

Not blackbird or thrush
in a startled trajectory of flight.

Not pigeon, undecided which way
that way, this or where to go

nor seagull, taking careful note
of make and registration for later.

This scrap of feathers, beak
and eye orphaned on the road

didn't fly into my windscreen;
nor would I feel the impact,

only the stillness of his heartbeat
during quiet moments of the day.

Crash

It survived day-to-day
uses and abuses, pots
hot from the stove,

knives chopping away,
chance close encounters
with tap or sink. Onions

couldn't reduce it to tears.
Then a moment caught it
side on at a weak spot

we didn't know was there.
Sometimes things shatter
and leave us bereft

our faces stupid, stunned
behind the crazed glass.

Breakdown

Bad enough to break down
and be towed facing the way
you want to go, slowed
by mechanical inertia
yet still moving forward;

but who'd want to be towed
backwards, in reverse, away
from what you thought
was your destination, which gets
sucked back into the distance
as you watch

and where you came from,
where you are now going,
is only visible in the rear view mirror,
the size of a holiday postcard
you thought you'd posted long ago.

Last Chance

Leven, Fife is nowadays a frontier town in modern
east of Scotland style. Imaginary tumbleweed
is blown by North Sea winds that taste of salt

along the dual carriageway and past Banbeath
Industrial Estate. Some mornings you can almost hear
the rumble of the iron horse which used to ride this trail.

Now only Stagecoach battles through. The tourists come
to mosey down the Promenade where one-armed-bandits
still hold sway. Of course, the 'Indians' are take-aways

but cowboys roam from door to door and drive hard deals
in double glazing. Meantime for the good, the bad
and others back on Main Street, music loud with drink

spills out of each saloon while cash tills play a tune
which sure ain't Bluegrass. Fivers by the fistful
buy you burgers, chips or the latest brand-name trainers

(except for line dancers, no-one here wears cowboy boots).
Still, it's a wilderness beyond the forty-mile speed limit.
Night draws down the shutters and we circle round

our digital TVs, tune out the wild coyote call. But if you dare
to head out west where dust clouds gather
on the ridge, check the neon sign. It says:

Last petrol to the Forth Road Bridge
Last petrol to the Forth Road Bridge

Nova Scotia

He's fat, bald, mid-fifties, with a short beard
and earrings, exudes an air of menace
nicely wrapped. *Aw right if I sit here?*
He winks, and the guard blows her whistle.
It's August, festival time. He and I
have both left venues where others are still
enjoying an evening out beneath the red glow
of heaters warming up our northern sky.

From a Marks and Spencer's carrier bag
he offers smoked salmon and *a soft
little Chardonnay—hail the rotten fruit!*
—if I don't mind drinking from the bottle.
He's going home to Dundee. *Aberdeen?
Even seagulls can't afford to eat there.*

Women at Fifty

—After 'Men at Forty' by Donald Justice

Women at fifty
have just noticed the time.
They abandon the iron
to stamp its hoofbeats

across wrinkled shirts
and rush round the house
chucking into cupboards
clutter they won't need again:

whole decades fading
into dog-eared photographs,
letters with lots of love,
a far away beach sinking

into the blue recycling bin.
Cheap wine is a hangover
poured down the sink
and while empty bottles clink,

the smell of last night's dinner
dances with dust motes in the air.
Lipstick in one hand, a comb
in the other, one sensible shoe off

or on, *diddle, diddle, dumpling,*
one eye on the clock,
they race through the house
grabbing keys, purse, phone.

Flushed, take one last look
in the mirror, shrug.
Women at fifty
slam doors shut.

The Scottish Chip

David Annand's bronze sculpture of the 18thcentury poet
Robert Fergusson stands outside Canongate Church on
the Royal Mile, Edinburgh.

Chips, remnants of a lost lunch, lie scattered
around Robert Fergusson's feet and mine,
where a pigeon grabs at them, tossing them
like cabers. This grey feathered athlete
is an added attraction for school parties
and middle-aged women. They pause for photo
opportunities beside me and the statue—
Get your hands out of his pockets, Eileen!
—en route for Holyrood. The bird carries on
regardless, eye to the main chance, seeing off
any rivals venturing too close. Throwing
his weight around, he stabs and tosses away.
Chips fly around the poet's head, and mine,
as this sassy, wee cock-of-the-walk hurls
his dwindling stock. This pigeon has no chip
on his shoulder, though soon Fergusson and I do.

v.

now it starts
a stir of soft maracas
as the trees let go

In the Mort House

On calm nights when the sky
slips down to drape the land in black,
behind the Mort House shutters
in an outer room the widower
keeps watch; and heat from two fires
cannot stop his shivering. Beyond
the lath-and-plaster white partition
those grim sisters, time and sweet
decay, work on relentlessly
to beat the body snatchers
at their game.

His ears alone can hear
the resurrection men steal out
from earth's dark folds,
boots scraping sparks,
spades finding stone,
then earth, then flesh
wrapped bone.

Monks Bar, York

No public finale
for the unfortunates
who climbed
these winding steps.
No comfort
in the open skies
above, or friends
who came to stand
and watch. Here
there's barely room
to swing an axe.
No onlookers, just stones
soaking up prayers
through centuries
of final words

                        and pigeons
nesting up against
the old glass of the window slit,
indifferent to humankind
within. An arm's reach
from the execution block,
the parent bird looks
only at her nestling.
New life huddles
in a clutch of dirt
and feathers,
tender-beaked.
Above its head,
a glimpse of sky.

Bird in the Hand, Fleetingly

Bones and trees can last for centuries.
Give them a hill-top vantage point,
they'll watch as generations come and go
till science cuts them up to count the rings
or grinds them down to make fine china.
Cups unearthed from graves have outlived lips
which sipped from them, and ancient hands
intact in every bony detail shrug off time.

Compared to wood or bone, the spirit
is a short-stay visitor; but while a tree
through all its years may nurse ten thousand
tiny hearts, each skeleton remembers only one.
Nor does the bird who builds her nest
amongst the branches think she owns the tree.

Another Life

like to the swift flight of a sparrow through the room
wherein you sit
                        —The Venerable Bede

Left alone up there in the dark
the starling would have gone
quietly, huddled against a box
of Christmas decorations,

a few late flutterings causing
tiny bells to ring out of season,
the iridescence of his wings
fading to a dusty black.

But we threw open the hatch,
rattled the Ramsay ladder
and startled him into wild panic.

Nothing straightforward
about his sojourn here
except that final mad flight.

At 87

Imperfect or perfect,
historic or not,
she can't remember dinner,

never mind our visit yesterday.
The past in all its forms
and personal conjunctions

is going, going, gone.
The future's out of sight
beyond a hush of curtain.

Living in the present tense
(this moment—now—today)
she sleeps though most of it.

The Visit

i.m. Margaret Barton

That day, I found you
tiny in the bedroom chair,
translucent skin as soft
as moths' wings, lit up
like a paper lantern.

I brought you tight
curled hyacinths,
cut lilac sweet
to scent the room.

Three days later
you were gone.
Even the hyacinths
outlasted you.

Handed Down

i.m. William A.B. Ritchie

Your long piano fingers
charmed the peel from apples
and on Sunday mornings
picked out hymns.
Steering wheels moved
smoothly to their touch.

My hands are not like yours,
no similarity in skin or bone.
But in the driver's seat,
when courtesy requires
a hand signal and I wave,
it's your gesture, thrown away.

even metaphor
fades away

and the power station lum
will soon follow

all those
who ever climbed it

Notes on the Poems

Eleanor Livingstone's experience of childhood asthma is referenced in some of these poems.

'The Witchfinder's Daughter', p.23
Witchfinders employed needles on those accused of witchcraft, trying to find a 'devil's spot' where they didn't feel pain.

'The Soul', p.35
This poem responds to Don Paterson's Afterword to 'Orpheus' in which he writes that Rilke said of dogs 'we have raised them up to a soul for which there is no heaven'.

'1973', p.44
'Sylvia' is an instrumental track by the Dutch band Focus.

'*Sic Transit*', p.50
In Greek mythology, Artemis is goddess of the moon.

'The Snowman', p.58
'Rosie Bright' was a high quality coal from the Rosie Pit in Wemyss, Fife.

'In the Mort House', p.73
Mort houses are where the dead were kept in graveyards to prevent the theft of bodies for medical research.

Acknowledgements

Versions of some of these poems previously appeared in
the following print and online anthologies, magazines and
journals: *Magma, Orbis, Envoi, The SHop, Fourteen, In the Event
of Fire* (New Writing Scotland, 2009), *Dreamcatcher, The Eildon
Tree, The Interpreter's House, Snakeskin, Unsuitable Companions*
(Happen*Stance*, 2007), *Seam, Fringe of Gold* (Birlinn, 2008),
Markings, Mslexia, Obsessed by Pipework, Smiths Knoll, Chapman
and *Weyfarers*.

A version of 'Night Watch' won the Second Light 2008
competition.

Thanks to Happen*Stance* Press who published two pamphlets,
The Last King of Fife (2005) and *A Sampler* (2008), in which
some of the poems here originally appeared; also to Nell
Nelson, Karen Doherty, Jim Carruth and Sheila Wakefield
for advice and support in putting together this collection in
2010 and 2023.

A NOTE ON THE TYPE

This volume is set in Bembo Book, a digital updating
of the classic Renaissance typeface by Francesco Griffo.
Earlier digital versions of Bembo lacked the weight
and solidity of the old letterpress typeface; Bembo
Book aims to replicate, in a digital environment,
the robustness of the latter. Bembo is a beautiful,
time-honoured typeface eminently suited to
a large range of uses for print, not least poetry.